Past Life Regression

Exploring The Past to Heal The Present

Karen E Wells

Past Life Regression

Copyright

Table of Contents

Contents

Dedication

To Jo; whose love, support, endless patience, laughter, tears and our journey through life together has enabled me to take the steps needed and without whom I would be totally lost. I love you more than words will ever convey.

To Lula; my darling girl whose smile lights up my whole world and being, your presence in our lives has been enriched beyond anything I could have ever imagined. Thank you for choosing us, I love you through all the universe's and back....always.

To my family; This life together has been a journey, an eye opener, a wonder at the marvel of the human. Thank you for choosing me and giving me the gifts to step forward once again.

My friends; Here are we again, at another special time in the evolution of life. Many times before and without doubt again. You are a sea of calm in a wild storm and for that I am forever thankful!

To Mike Robinson & Jo Le-Rose; Your love has shown me the way home and blessed was I the day I met you both. Lost, afloat on the sea of despair but no longer, you heard my cry and stepped forward as you have many times before; my eternal gratitude & love to you both.

To The One; You never left, I just never knew until I finally awoke.

To Annette; Without you this book would not be possible, thank you so much.

And to all my clients & students that have over the years walked through my door wherever I have been in the world and shared their soul with me. Without you this book could not be written, I have been truly blessed to have been a part of your experience and your sharing. Thank you.

For many years Karen has been privileged to work with the most amazing clients' around the world. Each person that has walked through her door has had an amazing story to tell from deep within their soul. This book details some of the stories that have been shared with Karen whilst her client's have been under Hypnosis experiencing their past lives.

The book has been written to show how powerful this work can be and also to show that past lives are real and can be affecting each of us in many different ways as you will see in the case studies shown within this book. Perhaps it will open the heart of the reader to experience their own journey and to understand all that they have been before and will be again.

May the winds of love guide you to the essence of who you really are.

Author's Note

The job of a Past Life Regression therapist can be enlightening & captivating as you direct your clients back in time, hundreds and thousands of years ago to uncover aspects of themselves that need healing.

As a therapist doing this work, we are often looking for repeating patterns and by simply exploring those, seeing, feeling and healing what happened in the past, this can be enough to enable any client to heal and move on.

Having regressed thousands of clients over the years, I have seen physical, emotional and mental blockages heal bringing light to their current life.

Some people become apprehensive about past lives and uncovering those for themselves. It's important to put things into perspective and to know that they are just memories – things in the past that happened that we simply just want to let go off. It's that easy, it's that simple.

I have been incredibly blessed that this large number of souls have stepped forward onto my path, each client learning and providing a wonderful experience for me and for that I am so thankful. I have been teaching other therapists these techniques for some years so that they can go en-masse out into the world and help their clients. It is a privilege.

It's a fascinating subject and one that can be talked about for hours and hours, days and days. There is no element of religion, no belief system, just a gentle knowing and trusting from the client about what is right for them.

I have not been a therapist drawn by the fact of famous past lives – it does not matter to me who people have been but more their journey. I have shared a tiny proportion of my sessions with clients in this book just to give you an understanding of this work and how patterns can reoccur.

What matters most is this very present moment – this moment right now – when you listen to your heartbeat inside and all goes still and silent – that is the space of what we know in a spiritual sense to exist. It's that connection, that quiet power that when listened to, moves you into life's great journey and what a journey that can be.

Karen E. Wells

Introduction

In modern society, there are so many demands on life and over time, your experiences shape you; with layers accumulating as you progress on your journey through life. Even with the best guidance, it can be difficult to retain true perceptions or behaviours, let alone to heal any emotional or physical traumas experienced en-route. There's no doubt that while on your journey in this life, each emotional experience and angst will weigh heavily impacting and forming the dominant patterns right now. Whether you believe in the possibility of past lives or are simply curious, consider that the prospect is real and as such, it adds new dimensions to the way that you think and act.

Past life therapy provides a direct route towards accessing these origins, your origins and this information can be surprisingly useful helping with the healing of any issues experienced today. In fact, it is likely they are linked. Consider the impressions of any former lives as encoded within you, they form a template that impresses upon your physical and emotional state. Unfinished lessons from any former existence are also carried forward so it is not difficult to see how significant each experience is in life and why hypnosis and past life regression can be beneficial.

Past life regression is a pleasant, relaxing state of being; it is dream-like in essence but safe. The information that can arise from a session often provides many answers to issues that may have perplexed the individual for a long time. It can also open up the doorway to former lives which leads to research and feelings of completeness thereafter. This book is written in an informative way revealing all of the necessary information about hypnosis and past-life regression to pique your curiosity or, it could lead towards a wonderful new life as a therapist should this appeal.

Take advantage of the completely free Past Life MP3 here: http://karenewells.co.uk/mp3s/
Please enter the code PLRBOOK

Chapter One

What Is Hypnosis?

The key to freedom

is unlocking the subconscious.

Karen E Wells

With a history that spans the centuries, hypnosis is an often misunderstood therapy, surrounded by misconceptions arising through the public face and the drama of stage hypnotism. But hypnosis has no connection with the dramatics; it's a healing therapy, and one that provides a genuine and beneficial aid, assisting in the recovery of a wide range of conditions.

Hypnosis, simply, is a state of altered consciousness and is associated with relaxation and heightened suggestibility. The shift of awareness leads toward sleep but sleep is not actually experienced. Those under hypnosis are usually more predisposed to being open to suggestions than they might normally be. The ethos is that hypnosis can lead people towards identifying and resolving deeply rooted issues that may have caused problems in their lives for many years.

It's impossible to go through life without experiencing a full range of emotions and experiencing traumas whether in love, through betrayal, rejection or grief as a result of bereavement. Painful emotions are often stored within, buried, unresolved and hidden, where they can create significant damage if left. Through therapy, these unresolved issues can be discovered and subsequently healed.

The suggestions provided are an integral part of any therapy and although some people may feel it a little daunting initially, a qualified therapist will soon have the client feeling relaxed. It's important to realise that the client always remains in control at all times and can return to a conscious state at will.

Suggestions are more successful than direct statements of change and the therapist, once granted access through the subconscious mind; can apply suggestions that can take root implementing the start of any psychological or behavioural changes.

In spite of popular belief, hypnosis may not work for everyone. Some people are simply not susceptible to suggestion and the therapy will not work if the person does not voluntarily agree to treatment. It's also important to note that those who hold onto unconscious fears or, try too hard may not be able to access their past life memories, but this can be worked upon with the help of a good Regression therapist.

Great results can be achieved from just one session. This depends on the nature of the problem of course.

To be able to suggest life-style changes, ideas or concepts, the conscious mind is suppressed and the subconscious mind is then revealed and accessed. Consider hypnosis as a type of psychotherapy aiding in the reprogramming of existing behaviours, it is beneficial for many areas including anxieties, stress and negative beliefs.

The therapist reassures the client and then leads them gently into relaxation so that the session is nurturing and safe, eliminating any nervousness and allaying fears. The therapist may use a wide-range of techniques to achieve the required state: symbolism, metaphors or even guided imagery – all which must bear some relevance to the client. With past life regression, there is the potential to uncover problems from the client's past which may be impacting the present time, so that patterns of behaviours and issues can be healed and a shift towards a healthier experience can be realised.

Everyone experiences their journey into deep relaxation and into the altered state differently but the client remains fully in control throughout.

This deep, tranquil state is pleasant and enjoyable. Many people become aware of physical sensations around them and as a result, become much more in tune with their surroundings. Those who have endured deeply traumatic events and where their memory is limited or blocked find that hypnosis provides the key to unblocking these memories, aiding the healing process. The sensation feels similar to that sleepy in-between state - neither fully asleep nor fully awake. Clients may deem it as if a day-dream or trance and as people have often experienced similar trance-like states in life naturally, so the experience is not alarming at all.

The following conditions are often aided by hypnosis:

- Phobias
- Anxieties
- Depression
- Sleep Disorders
- Addictions
- Stress
- Bereavements
- Post-Traumatic Stress
- Pain Management
- Weight Control
- Public Speaking
- Sexual Dysfunction
- Eating Disorders
- Life Transitions
- Life Purpose
- Creative Blocks

Communication between the client and therapist is important. There has to be a feeling of trust and of rapport. The sessions are not unpleasant; there is nothing to fear but rather one of deep relaxation and of gentle support. Time is taken with a new client to establish medical history, general health and lifestyle and to ascertain the client's needs and goals. During hypnosis, communication extends where the therapist directs the client's thoughts and imagination in a way designed to change thoughts and feelings, increase sensation and to alter perceptions or behaviours.

Benefits of Hypnosis

The human mind is complex and when only the conscious mind is accessed, a mere 10% of the mind as a whole is treated. Therefore, hypnosis provides a vital tool to explore, to discover and to treat any underlying problems that exist in the other 90% of the subconscious mind. Memories that have been hidden and which may be responsible for holding the client back in life can be rediscovered.

Hypnosis is not just about overcoming problems, it can help to identify the true nature of the individual and to discover how and why experiences and beliefs may have played such an integral effect in life. There is the opportunity to eliminate sabotaging behaviours, to re-programme perceptions and to transform destructive habits into positive attitudes.

Many people also have a keen interest in regressing back through the years to childhood and beyond where secrets of past lives can be brought into the here and now.

Common benefits of typical hypnosis sessions include:

- Improving self-esteem and confidence
- Increasing communication skills
- Reducing stress and anxieties
- Promoting health and well-being
- Improving a sleep pattern
- Improving concentration and mental clarity
- Identifying negative thought patterns or behaviours and re-programming with positive concepts
- Eradicating resentments or the emotional pain of rejection

Types of Hypnosis

There are generally two types of hypnosis used and a therapist may specialise in one area or, a combination of techniques may be used depending on the client's response.

Traditional Suggestion

When traditional suggestion is used, the therapist puts the client into a deeply relaxed state of mind and then suggestions are planted into the subconscious mind. It will usually take several sessions for the suggestions to take place although once deeply rooted, the benefits may be experienced quite quickly. Traditional Suggestion is likely to be less effective on those clients who have an analytical nature.

Ericksonian Hypnosis

Once the client is in a relaxed state, metaphors are used to acquire the right result. It works because the subconscious brain which quickly understands the connection between the designated behaviour and the metaphor but the conscious brain becomes distracted by the metaphor. This enables the true meaning of the metaphor to access the subconscious mind directly. This type of hypnosis works very effectively on those people who are usually resistant to the prospect of hypnosis or, who have logical or analytical minds.

The Root of the Problem

Hypnosis is used to determine an effective solution as quickly and efficiently as possible. While some areas may need extensive sessions, the aim is to discover the root issue of the problem and to address it. Hypnosis isn't just about treating the symptoms although as a by-product of the treatment, symptoms will improve.

The aim of the therapist is to create a feeling of well-being for the client taking them into a state of altered consciousness enabling access to a much deeper level of awareness. The therapist will seek the underlying emotional cause which can materialise as emotional, psychosomatic or as psychological problems.

Through accessing these deeper levels of the mind, positive changes can be implemented, often through suggestion or, in some cases through metaphor, which will start the healing and behavioural transformations. The aim is to heal the client and to improve life on multiple levels. These aims are discussed at the start of the session and communication is important throughout.

Hypnosis has changed very little over the centuries but it is our understanding of it that has grown now that the many benefits have been established. The ability to use it to heal in multiple areas is astounding. Hypnosis, far from being dangerous or gimmicky is a highly beneficial therapy that does not seek to control or brainwash the mind, rather, it's a gentle, suggestive therapy that produces far-reaching, positive, healing effects.

Chapter Two

What Is Past-Life Regression?

Regression simply means – a journey back in time. We know that hypnotherapy is a safe and gentle way to overcome a great many issues but it is also the vehicle in which the past life journey begins. The client experiences a hypnotic induction including a deepening relaxation leading to a careful, suggested regression all the way back to pre-womb life. This is the time when a client may signify or identify with a former character and comments are drawn forward regarding physical elements or sensations experienced in a body which is not their own. In other words, there are often feelings, a description which may be of themselves or of a scene in which they have become involved. Some clients begin to experience flashbacks and very vivid memories - so a sequence of events occurs as it plays out.

So how does past life regression work?

The fundamental theory is one where your soul is reborn each time in a different body and possibly a different gender. If you consider that the soul may be infinite, then it's quite possible to have any number of past lives. There is a strong belief that life is similar to a school so there are important lessons to be learned each and every time. Whether the lessons are learned or not, one life will affect the next and thereafter until growth is achieved, the soul chooses each lesson in life to experience and everything is planned before the soul reincarnates.

The lessons that we each choose trigger growth so perhaps the human condition needs hardship of sorts to enable us to make wiser choices or to learn from mistakes made. One life may be infinitely harder than another but all souls are equal and with equal opportunities for growth. Sometimes the stumbling blocks to growth are caused by the individual through fear and through emotional blockages but this is an area in which past life regression can deftly deal with these stumbling blocks, creating a healing chain of events.

It's important to consider why anyone would wish to be regressed and the answers vary but include:

- To learn more about themselves spiritually
- To take greater responsibility for actions and behaviours
- To satisfy a curiosity caused through repeated déjà vu
- To heal emotionally and physically
- To identify engrained patterns
- To received guidance
- To receive answers
- To enrich the present

Lost memories can sometimes be triggered simply by visiting new places, by reading or even through dreams. Sometimes, an individual experiences an overwhelming certainty that they have been to a place before or, they have the strangest feeling that they've had a conversation before, the feeling can be disorientating as they fail to identify when. Similarly, déjà vu strikes again as they start to repeat the same series of events over and over.

There is the strongest sense of familiarity that bursts in and out of the conscious mind and these fragments of a life gone by can be overwhelming to say the least. Some people have a resurgence of memories through meditating or through their day dreams and memories can appear if involved in energy work. Those of a strong intuitive nature may have very clear memories of past lives and be totally accepting of it.

As we struggle to understand our place in this world, many people would like to believe in reincarnation as it opens up some wonderful possibilities. It's a comfort that they may have lived before but therein also lies the fear of what may have happened to them during those years. This uncertainty can cause some people to stop exploring their past lives but really there is nothing to be concerned about, in fact the opposite. Exploring the past can answer so many questions in the present day, it's a little like finding and placing the final pieces of a jigsaw puzzle. It all starts to make sense.

Those who have not experienced a regression are often concerned as to the potential severity of some memories especially if traumatic memories should resurge. It is true that some people do recall vivid recounts of dramatic or volatile circumstances and although this may appear to be distressing or even traumatic, it can also afford that individual great release and a sense of freedom.

A qualified past life regression therapist is also able to fully support and guide their clients through these deep and emotive regressions, enabling them to witness from a distance rather than to feel as if it is happening to them at that time.

If you are interested in having a regression, find a skilled and experienced regression therapist – one who knows how to word the suggestions so that valid memories can resurge but so that it limits unnecessary panic. When this happens, a skilled Past Life Regression therapist can calmly let the client go through the incident again enabling healing to take place or a therapist with not much experience can enable uncomfortable situations to be fast-forwarded until the client has moved past the emotion. It's easy to implant the suggestion of distance so that the client steps away from the intensity of the scene and begins to watch as the scene unfolds from a safer distance.

There's no doubt that some people are deeply moved by their former lives but most people find the experience rewarding beyond belief.

It helps them to feel a part of something bigger than they could have imagined and it makes sense of their piece of the puzzle.

The best results within past life regression is when a commitment to the process is made. Multiple sessions may work best because it takes time to build up good communication, rapport and of course trust. These are important elements as the individual must acquire the right state of mind. There is a limit to the amount of work that can be completed in just one session but it provides a wonderful introduction to anyone who wishes to understand the process and to peek through the fabrics of time.

There are a great many benefits of undergoing past life regression therapy and these include:

- Emotional growth
- Releasing traumas that have become root issues
- To discover previous talents and abilities and to utilize them in the present
- To renew or rediscover current relationships and improve behaviours
- To discover life's purpose
- To satisfy the need to know whether reincarnation is real
- To step back beyond the veil

Many people have discovered long forgotten talents through regression and have been able to make use of these instinctive talents going forward. These can be natural gifts, interests or skills and ones that you may have excelled in during a previous lifetime. These natural talents may be a surprise to you in this life but slip easily into your day to day life in an instinctive way.

This is just one of the benefits that can happen and it can add new depth to your life if you can allow it to become an extension of your life today.

If you are considering having a past life regression session, know that you may well witness these positive attributes when you step back in time and to make the most of each session, it's a good idea where possible to vocalise all that you are seeing, this provides a more detailed description for the therapist and for the recording of the session, providing greater proof and topics to discuss. Later it is possible to analyse the recording of the session and this adds credence to this element of proof.

In the early stages of regression, it can all seem a little overwhelming, there may be an abundance of imagery and noise around you and you'll feel a strong sense of anticipation as you merge into the character that you were before. It may seem impossible to make sense of the impressions initially, let alone to focus on personal traits such as skills. You will however find that it becomes less daunting as your sessions continue and you will be able to ascertain more information than you thought possible providing you approach regression with an open mind.

Consider the opportunity to witness your former life's events and to have a sneak preview of your personality at that time, how you may have looked and to witness your behaviours, identifying with those who play a part in your life at that time. No one can predict the amount of information that can come forward; even ill-health and details of your demise may come to light but this is not as difficult to deal with as it might sound.

Once you are relaxed within the sessions you may find yourself better able to open up into the mind of that former individual, you may experience deep thoughts, feelings and even movements. You may feel great joy or great sadness. Emotions are pure energy so they are strong enough to transverse time.

Chapter Three

Past Life Clues

Do you have a strong inclination that you have lived before? You are not alone if so, many people have a strong belief that reincarnation exists and hope to receive proof from a former life to enable them to have proof of this continuous cycle of existence. If you consider our presence on this planet, it does seem impossible that we would be limited to living for only a few decades in just one life, so with this in mind, it's worth delving back and finding out for yourself.

You may even have experienced potential clues to your past lives – there are unique indicators that can make you question your life today.

Déjà vu

Déjà vu is not unique; many will have experienced that feeling of familiarity at some point in their lives. But some people have very strong and sometimes frequent feelings of familiarity. They feel that they have experienced an event before, in fact, at the moment of déjà vu; the feeling is very strong within them. Déjà vu can happen at any time and without warning. People may feel they have been to a location before and even know the area geographically or they may feel that they've had the same conversation before. Often, the feeling dissipates upon analysis but this simply leads to that individual questioning the potential for past lives and wondering about theirs. There has long been research into neurological explanations but there is a strong drive towards déjà vu being indicative of lost memories surging to the fore.

Memories

In the western world, we do not encourage children with stories of reincarnation. If they recount tales of people or places that they could not possibly have seen, this is discouraged. It is the western culture to be disbelieving. Children will often have memories of events, places or people that cannot be and it is possible that children are far more able to recall memories of their former lives, although this ability usually dissipates with age.

Dreams

Recurring dreams and nightmares have long been considered a clue to a potential past life. Many dreams are caused through life events and through the brain being stimulated – a television program, a conversation or even a current problem that nags away while unresolved but some dreams could be indicative of a past life event. Similarly, nightmares can occur as a reflection of traumas once faced in a previous existence or at least depict the fear that surges forward as a result of difficult memories. Certainly those with a strong interest in past life regression consider that some dreams are valid reminders of a life gone by.

Habits

We all have bad habits – usually harmless but, uncontrolled habits or compulsions can take over an individual's life. Those with obsessive disorders or addictions in this lifetime could be feeling the weight of memories from through the veil where these behaviours may have occurred.

Aches and Pains

There is a line of thought that those everyday annoying aches and pains could actually be a sign of ill-health in a former life. An old injury or severe health condition then could resurface as a reminder. The only way to know for sure would be to take those steps toward a past life regression session where evidence of that life may come to the fore.

Birthmarks

Strange birthmarks have been added to the list as potential past life evidence. Details of the birthmarks have been shown under regression as have other physical traits. Some people have reported that their birthmark is at the exact spot where they were killed by a specific object in a past life.

Soul Mates

We all yearn to find that special one but if you have already found your soul mate, what is it about them that connect you both on such a deep, emotional and spiritual level? Did you meet them and instantly recognise them on a sub-conscious level? You may have close friends who you have felt you have known all of your life and yet, realistically, it's only been for a short time - certainly in this life and yet, that familiarity and bond is strong. There is a theory that we find groups of people, reacquainting ourselves with them throughout our journeys. We meet up with our family members, friends and lost loved ones and identify with them on an instinctive level. This is known as soul recognition.

Many people like to travel but some become obsessed with the culture of other lands. They search through history, identify with the people who have lived there and during the relevant time and feel as if they truly 'belong' there. Is there some rational explanation or could they have lived in that country during one lifetime?

Egypt – A Huge Fascination.

A lot of people have a fascination with Egypt. Egypt was such an amazing time in the history of the world and Ancient Egypt was a civilisation that lasted over 5000 years. Whether you believe in past lives or not, the chances are you may have had a Past Life in Ancient Egypt.

Here are a few clues that may indicate that you could have had a Past Life at this time:

- Do you have a fascination with a particular Pharaoh or time period in Egypt's history, for example – Cleopatra, Nefertiti, Ramses II, Hatshepsut?

- Have you been to Egypt and experienced Déjà vu in one of the temples or places like Karnak, Luxor Temple or the Pyramids at Giza?

- Have you always had an interest in Egypt, reading every book you can or watching every movie or documentary on it?

- Do you have emotional reactions to certain events or times within Ancient Egypt's history?

All of these things could indicate you have had a Past Life in Egypt.

As part of who we are, we carry energy of past lives with us and these reactions as stated above can often indicate that the energy of that life is still with us. Maybe there is something from that life that needs to be cleared, or maybe it's just to remind you of a wonderful, affluent time in your own history, who knows? Ancient Egypt holds a fascination for many people and the answers are there within ourselves.Can you take the leap and journey inside to reveal your past?

Does any of this sound familiar to you? If you experience déjà vu, have strange recollections or dreams, it's certainly worth making a note of them so that they are not forgotten; this can be especially useful following past life regression sessions where some of the information that comes to light may correlate with the information you already have listed. This can spark off the need to research more and to don the role of a past life detective finding out who you were and all that happened to you.

Chapter Four

Belonging In The Past

Do you have the strangest sensation that you may have lived in a specific time period? Perhaps you feel drawn to the 1930's or 1940's? Perhaps you have a strong feeling that you lived in another country and your heart is connected to the people and place more than to your current home environment. Although we've mentioned this in the previous chapter, it's worth noting that this happens to great many people. While the connection could have occurred through material read or programs reviewed that has sparked off the imagination, many people have found themselves wondering about the possibility of a past life as their passion about the past is an interest that fails to wane.

This isn't just a simple preference for a bygone era or a liking for the style of clothes or the lifestyle at that time, it can be a deeply rooted almost obsessive attachment to this period which translates into a need to collect items that represent the time or place. As a result, there can be a sense of peace through having those possessions nearby.

Sometimes, there is an overpowering familiarity in the language used or being drawn to the style of clothes and this can be significant of past memories, enough to make you wonder. It's possible to be drawn to something that has its roots firmly placed in history without even realising why.

Unrealistic fears or phobias can also be indicative of fears that existed in a past life, especially when there appears to be no reason for them to exist.

Have you chosen to live in a house which has all the period features and is steeped in history? Perhaps you have furnished your house, blending elements of old and new and this becomes a comfort, a tenuous link to the past that retains the familiarity. These are indicators that are not just borne out of curiosity and if you consider the time period, would you really like to step back in time? What is it that draws you to that era? There may be moments in history that seem significant to you, there may be moments in history that repel you and fill you with an uneasy sense of familiarity.

With past life regression, the journey back through lives means the necessity of encountering good and bad memories and being able to embrace vivid images as they occur. It does take a certain amount of bravery to face the unknown but it can offer so many benefits if this course is taken.

Embracing the truth is an important element of past life regression.

Have you ever experienced déjà vu? You may have visited a location and have experienced the strongest sense of familiarity. Fleeting impressions may bombard your senses as you walk around, you may even instinctively know the right direction to move in, even though you are sure you have never been there before. It can be disconcerting to feel this deep recognition without fully understanding why.

In the same way, you might meet someone for the very first time and yet, you feel as if you have known them forever. You might struggle to know why this occurs, recognising something about them but knowing that you have never met. It is possible that you have known them throughout a former life. Certainly déjà vu can be a pleasurable experience especially when encountering something that brings a sense of warmth into your life. But it's important to note déjà vu can also represent a warning perhaps to help you avoid a situation may have happened in the past.

There is no way of controlling déjà vu, it can certainly happen at any time and in any place and it occurs unbidden. The simplest moment can trigger something deep within your unconscious memory and this blast from the past can come surging to the fore. How many times have you had déjà vu? If it has happened on more than one occasion, perhaps it is time to listen and to consider whether there has been a pattern to the experiences. Did they involve the same people occurring in a certain place and were there others with you during those times?

Suddenly, from nowhere comes the realization that you have had the same conversation before. More, it feels as if you have lived this moment. When these moments occur, look around, make a note of who you were with and the conversation, this might be important in past life regression research.

Many people have re-occurring dreams, ones that are still vivid even upon waking. Your conscious mind takes a break during sleep and so your experiences recent and beyond exist within your unconscious mind, sometimes something triggers a memory, it could be a conversation, something that you have witnessed, but even the smallest trigger can spark off a forgotten moment from your past life. Eventually, the memory filters into your mind and the story plays out, fading as you enter a conscious state or sometimes remaining.

Dreams occur in a multitude of ways - they can be inspired by events witnessed with interwoven stories that are easily deciphered, but dreams can also appear to have little relevance too. The idea, the concept, can appear muddled and non comprehensive or so realistic in that it echoes aspects of your life now. The characters within that dream may be familiar, perhaps you recognise them on an intrinsic level but they act out a different role in this dream. Sometimes dreams are simply the ramblings of the mind but sometimes it relates to a psychic insight. You may dream out a scenario and then later, the dream becomes reality. Dreams can be symbolic too and they can be fanciful, containing elements with strong emotional undercurrent that replay over and over.

Lucid dreams can also continue after waking and it is possible to re-enter the confines of the dream and see the outcome while retaining control.

If while reading this, you find that it makes sense and you have experienced recurring dreams seemingly disconnected from your daily life, then it is worth keeping a dream journal and jotting down any of the dreams experienced so you don't forget them. Whether you believe in the potential for past lives or not, it will give you a unique insight as to whether anything is troubling you. This may be anxieties that remain hidden and unresolved. A journal will also indicate recurring patterns that develop within the dreams and these can become real indicators towards a former life.

Here's an example of the type of information you should collate in your dream journal:

- Who played a part in your dream?
- What happened in the dream?
- What was the location?
- Have you had this dream before?

It's important to add in any details that you think necessary as dreams are certainly a window to the subconscious mind and could be the gateway to a past life.

Chapter Five

Past Lives – Fantasy Or Reality

Past Lives – Fantasy or Reality? The number one question on everyone's lips!

How do you know if past lives are real? Is it likely that when you undergo a regression, you could be Henry VIII, Cleopatra, Mary Magdalene or even Jesus? Are those souls alive on the Earth today….? Through many years of regressing clients' back into their past lives, most people have lived ordinary, normal lives like we live today (sorry Jesus if that's you!)

However, that is not to say that occasionally as a Regression Therapist, a client may come through your door and share with you the most amazing past life of theirs that you can both investigate afterwards and discover the truth of their words through research.

So, how do you know if past lives are a reality or a fantasy? The thoughts & feelings that can occur in a regression session can be intense and these are not something that can be "imagined" by the conscious mind. Imagining something happening is not the same as really experiencing something. Anyone can imagine a certain scenario but to experience the scenes, the dramas, and the interactions in a regression session is completely different – they feel real.

Some client's come with a desire to be someone important. I have regressed 2 separate people who both believed they were Mary Magdalene. Whilst it is impossible for 2 separate people to be the same soul that was Mary Magdalene, it was obvious from my consultation with one of the client's that this was a fantasy wish of theirs and not a reality. It did make for an enlightening session but not for the reasons that the client wanted!

So, if you are thinking about having a past life regression session yourself, it is possible you will uncover an ordinary life with ordinary circumstances. But you may have had amazing past lives that could have occurred at the time of these famous people, and this could have sparked your interest in them and in that time period. Or you could be that person….who knows? All answers are held within the subconscious mind; regression is the key to finding out for yourself.

Regression as a tool – helping clients' go deeper

As Hypnotherapists, we are taught to help our clients in many ways. There are many different techniques a Hypnotherapist can use to help someone who may come in with a variety of issues. Each client is different and many of the issues they present to you as a Hypnotherapist often overlap.

Our profession in Hypnotherapy generally leans towards helping clients using Suggestion Therapy. This is the easiest and most common way to help a number of issues. However, Suggestion Therapy can metaphorically speaking be likened to long blades of grass in a field (each issue presenting themselves as that blade of grass).

In order to successfully treat any client – a therapist has to dig out the roots of the grass – and the way to find these roots is to use Regression. Here are some vital points that show how Regression can help:

- Through Regression, the client is able to go back to vital points in their life in order to see where their issues stem from

- Regression is a quick & dynamic tool enabling the therapist to guide the client back to events in this lifetime or past lives

- Learning the process of Regression is often not enough. The therapist has to know what to do with the client once they are back in those memories in order to heal them

- Specialised healing techniques when used with Regression helps to heal presenting problems that clients' may have been carrying around for years and lifetimes

- Without Regression, the issue if treated by Suggestion Therapy is likely to come back at some point and present itself in the same way or as a different issue to the client.

Many therapists and clients have noted that within a single or a low number of sessions of Regression Therapy, more have healed within than by having weeks, months or years of different therapies.

It's important to never underestimate the wonder of huge improvements occurring with the client's well being from having had only limited amounts of time in any session.

Why your imagination is different to your past life memories

When someone comes for a Past Life Regression session, one of the main questions they ask is:

How do I know I'm not making it up or that it's not just my imagination?

Here are 5 Reasons why your imagination is different to your past life memories:

- Imagination can create a lot of things – think for a moment about something that you desire – that image can seem distant and without emotion. Now remember a childhood memory – see the difference in this – and notice the emotion linked with this. A real memory combined with emotion can feel like an explosion of things within you.

- When you thought of something you desired – did you feel it around your head? When you thought of a childhood memory or any memory – often the feeling comes from your heart – do it again and notice the difference.

- Often in a Past Life Regression intense emotion can come up out of nowhere – this could be from a number of reasons but the important thing is that the mind and the imagination are unable to create the intense feelings that often arise in a Regression session.

- The imagination will often want to conjure up an elaborate story – to imagine you were once perhaps Cleopatra or Jesus – when in fact most past lives that are explored reveal ordinary lives with ordinary circumstances.

- Past Life Memories often involve physical feelings – for example someone may begin to experience physical aches or pains from that Past Life – and again that is something the imagination cannot do.

So if you are thinking of exploring one or more of your past lives – the imagination is nothing to worry about. In the hands of the right Regression therapist, time travel to your past lives is possible and enlightening.

Chapter Six

The Healing Aspects Of Past Life Regression

For anyone new to past life regression, it may seem a little odd that by exploring the potential for any past lives, that it can also have a profound healing effect in the here and now. Past life regression has been shown to heal trapped emotions and painful traumas that may not even have been experienced in this lifetime and it does this by uncovering those deepest, darkest foundations of soul enabling you to release and forgive where necessary.

Although revealing secrets of those former lives may be traumatic depending on the situation that is revealed, it provides wonderful healing opportunities and can often offer closure to some painful, buried emotions. It also affords a greater sense of feeling connected; a life within many lives and provides reassurance.

We all grow in emotional maturity at varying speeds; and some people are simply not ready to explore their past life potential. Some remain stuck in the past, holding tightly onto drama and emotional pain without awareness. Others are prepared to face up to their experiences in life – and to experience both the good and bad memories, keen to understand their actions or behaviours. This positive approach enables those people to avoid being partially stuck in the traumas of any former life.

True healing occurs when each and every one of us learn to recognise the responsibility we have for our own lives and by doing so, find it easier to let go of any inner turmoil and to simply move forward into a life of greater positivity.

It is impossible to go through life without experiencing great joy and great emotional pain; it is part of the journey, but the strength of these emotions, good and bad often transverse into a physical reality.

Think of those times when you have felt great attraction or warmth for somebody, your heart flutters, your stomach twists in knots, you feel it deep within, so it's easy to see that your emotions can be incredibly strong in the present but these emotions can also endure from one lifetime to another.

The energy that we feel is very pure and energy fluctuates, it is free-flowing, its very nature is for change. But for many, this energy becomes blocked often through unresolved situations.

It's so important to face up to even the most hurtful of situations when we encounter them in life and to understand them, dealing fully with the pain before moving on. For some, shutting down those emotions and locking the event away deep within only allows it to fester and to resurface at some point, often manifesting in physical ways. As people become aware of past life regression, more and more people take the decision to seek out a qualified therapist in a bid to turn back the clock and to rediscover former identities and unresolved issues that could be responsible for disease or physical weaknesses in the present.

The human condition means that we are meant to feel.

We are meant to experience life in all of its glory. It is not possible to take shortcuts with emotions without damaging future experiences or experiencing behavioural issues or, physical problems as a result. If this life is all about learning important lessons, bypassing the experience blocks the opportunity to grow.

In a perfect life, there would be no emotional disharmony and it would be easy to recover from grief, from broken hearts or from traumatic events but it is only by becoming emotionally brave and working through this ever fluctuating emotional state that we are able to heal. Failure to move forward simply means being stuck in an ever rotating cycle of difficulties and of being tied to unresolved issues in this life or former lives.

Many clients have felt extraordinary release once the root cause of their problems has been discovered and deeply rooted issues are surprisingly not always complicated. Because we shut down the emotion as a way of protecting ourselves, it is often just a matter of facing up to the circumstances and the emotions and recognising that it exists. Time does the rest. Hiding from an emotional reality is not the solution.

Unresolved issues trigger off painful and unpleasant responses. Often, the simple process of past life regression can be enough to reveal the client's true reality, to make them aware of emotional blockages and to trigger off important memories from those former lifetimes and this awareness begins the healing process.

Past life therapy does not have to be complicated.

For some people, regression takes longer. Fear can prevent progress taking place and emotionally frozen, these people are incapable at that time to fully face up to whatever memories unfold. This is common, but once overcome, the rewards are extraordinary. Other clients are fully ready to explore their past lives and keen to understand why they think or act in certain ways in their present life, convinced that some of their behavioural patterns may have been caused as a result of living before. They are keen to express their emotions and to explore the obstacles that may have littered their route through a former life and to correlate these experiences with the present. Often, there is a direct link typically because emotions remained unexpressed and situations unresolved.

Each person is different and so their journey into the depths of past life regression will be unique to them but when guided by a competent past life therapist who is able to control the journey, and to guide them through, this serves to ensure the client steps neatly through a myriad of sometimes complex and painful memories. This may enable them to witness in detail without being engulfed by the intensity of any situation.

How the mind works

The mind is truly complex and is capable of many things. It can work for us or against us depending on whether we allow fear and negativity to rule, or, if we take a positive approach to life. If you consider that every time you search for a memory and bring it to the fore, in essence, you are taking that memory out of your unconscious mind. Some people replay unhealthy memories over and over even unwittingly and this certainly influences their actions on a day to day basis.

Some people imagine negative events happening before they do and therefore project an unhealthy memory into the future by capturing and utilising it unnecessarily and this casts a shadow over the present and future. But the mind is unique and no two people will ever witness an occurrence in the same way and this is because we all use our senses in an individual manner, even how we analyse and then recall a situation. Our perceptions can be tainted depending on our ability to translate the information around us but even these scenarios can be impacted by the lingering memories of past lives.

There are four basic patterns of brain wave cycles and these include:

- Alpha
- Beta
- Theta
- Delta

When we are wide awake and in a conscious state, this is known as beta. When we are in the beta brain wave cycle we are able to analyse problems or, study and we can organise information or make judgements. The delta brainwave cycle happens once we are asleep but it is the two patterns that occur between conscious wakefulness and sleep-brain wave cycle that are associated with hypnosis. In a past life regression session, the cycle of brainwaves slow down and the individual enters an alpha state which is known as a mild hypnotic state. As an example, this is the same brainwave level that we would enter naturally when we are deeply relaxed, reading or when engrossed in a good film.

The Alpha cycle occurs many times throughout the day often without anyone realising. Many people are surprised to understand that this state of hypnosis is such a familiar sensation where although you are involved in a film or book you may still be aware of movement nearby and your senses may still engage noises or sudden movement although your emotions will be connected with the task at hand.

Then there is the deeper level of hypnosis known as Theta and this is where the brainwave cycle slows down even more, going into a very natural and comfortable state, much of the past life regression work is done at this point. Those people who reach the theta stage tend to remember their regression experience more vividly.

Research has indicated however that throughout a past life regression there will be fluctuating brainwave patterns throughout.

Chapter Seven

Embrace The Past To Heal the Future

Karma is much talked about in past life regression as it makes sense of the cycle of lives and of the many experiences that have to be dealt with throughout the various journeys. People learn from this understanding of how their behaviours can reap negative rewards not necessarily in the same lifetime but, at some point. Whether the negative elements are aimed at them or caused by them, there will be karmic retribution. This knowledge might serve to act as a guiding element in life.

Think of regression as an opportunity to witness the results from actions or experiences in the past so they can be avoided in the present. It is like having friends help you through the complexities of life and to help you to avoid making the same old mistakes, only this time it's on a much more personal basis.

The cycle of karma means that whatever we have done to others in a past life, it will at some point occur again whether in this lifetime or in a future lifetime. It may take generations before that soul learns the true understanding of the pain caused at that time. The lesson is then learned. So karma provides a sense of cosmic justice but karma also rewards.

If you consider your desire for anything in life, what are your motives? Are you helping others because you feel a genuine need to do so or do you have a different motive? True good intent creates positive karma, so what you think and what you do is important. Everything that happens to you in life is down to you, so yes, even events that are unpleasant or hurtful. You have to take responsibility for decisions made and to be ready to learn the lessons that come your way in life.

Sometimes you create circumstances that test your resolve, it's your need, that of your soul and therefore, if we look at this in its truest form, there are no victims, it's all about balance. While your conscious mind will not welcome any arduous tests, the soul needs to be evaluated for growth. So in many ways, when you face the most difficult moments in life, they occur for a reason and how you deal with them will have a long lasting effect, you will carry unresolved issues from this point and into any future lives. The solution is to recognise the undulating twists and turns of life, and as much as we would all like the path-way to be smooth, the reality is that unexpected events and people have an effect on us. We must go of past mistakes, regret, guilt, anger or a desire for revenge. Without this, you will simply be in cycle of repeating bad relationships, bad situations and the same old negative conversations possibly with the same people.

Sometimes there is an 'Aha' moment, when we finally realise what life is all about. Past life regression can help.

But karma affects us all in multiple ways so even though some actions are cruel beyond belief – consider murder as an example, karma also evaluates every action however small. But it is important to realise that even if during a regression session that memories of bad past deeds begin to resurface and these deeds were committed by you, it does not mean to say that you will repeat the events in the present or in the future. You have a choice.

Blocks occur as a result of unresolved issues. In a past life regression session, blocks also occur where progress can be frustratingly slow. They can hinder the true outcome, but it is more important to realise that it is a temporary frustration sometimes occurring through an inability to make sense of the information received or an inability to validate the information.

As with everything in life, people develop or adapt to situations on an individual level. Some people may be slower to adapt to the regression process than others and therefore it can take a while before any images or information start to appear. Providing a client begins to trust the therapist and to relax into the session, progress will be made.

Some people can feel very self-aware and even a little silly at the start. It may take some time to let go of this self-conscious behaviour and to relax into hypnotherapy and the whole process of regression. It usually improves as the relationship between the therapist and the client becomes relaxed and the client is able to see that the sessions are non-judgemental.

It is harder for the client to stay in the trance if the analytical part of the mind is metaphorically closing the door to the past. By contrast, some people are so desperate for a result that this can form blocks while others appear to be almost reluctant to receive evidence of a former life and therefore, the blocks are neatly stacked in place.

The best way to approach what could be a healing session is to have an open mind.

People often associate past life regression with those stunning revelations of life as someone who played an important part in history or as a celebrity of the day, but this is rare. In fact, some people have such great expectations of revealing wondrous and exciting past events that they end up experiencing or remembering very little.

People approach past life regression in a very different way and when there are more significant details coming to the fore, it can be difficult for that person to make sense of the sudden surge of emotions and the images witnessed and in fact, it can be difficult to process. Some people will gloss over the traumas experienced, an unwillingness to see or act out certain aspects of their former life, and in fact, there can appear to be gaps within the information received. This can be because the individual has avoided dealing with any events that may be unpleasant or equally, the person may show a distinct detachment.

Understandably there may be individuals who are not prepared to deal with a past life trauma and if they are not ready for the healing process begin, it cannot be forced. If we consider that reincarnation is about finding the soul's true purpose and learning from mistakes made to be able to reach the full potential throughout life, it may be that this individual is not far enough into the journey. Where there are traumas and sadness, it is important to note that only the events that can be handled will surface.

Success depends on the approach and the ability to be guided and to see regression as a wonderful tool to be able to link the former lives together in a conscious manner.

Patterns of Behaviour

Once the process of past life exploration begins, you may be surprised to discover regularly repeated patterns that have occurred not just in this lifetime but in fact, could be centuries-old. This constant repetition starts to become familiar and so deeply engraved within, that you may not necessarily be aware of these elements. Of course past life regression sessions and the patterns that emerge are varied and they may be difficult to decipher in the first instance especially if someone is new to past life regression. These patterns can manifest as physical ailments, fears or even as tainted perceptions.

Although the information that comes to light will not always be negative, they are likely to be the ones that stand out as the strength of the emotions attached to them can carry forward throughout time. If someone in a regression session has experienced a very difficult, traumatic and perhaps violent relationship in this life, it's easy to wonder if they may attract a 'type' of person or that they act in a way that allows them to become the victim or, the abuser – depending on the situation. It's useful to note that these recurring patterns could have spanned the centuries and have endured in every lifetime to date.

Understanding that this behaviour is so deeply ingrained within can offer a great deal of relief as well as a sense of disbelief in that a shadowy past can play such a devastating part in the present.

The information received, however perceived can be taken in a positive way, because when you become aware of a recurring pattern, steps can be taken to eradicate it and, it is possible to change those behaviours going forward. This is a powerful and positive element within past life regression.

Some patterns of behaviour are positive and even the fact of having positive traits brought to life can be beneficial. But then there are the neutral patterns of behaviour that will not impact life in the same way, but, enriches the memory of the past life as it depicts softer, soothing memories of personality – for example; the person who loved nature, or, who was drawn to the mountains or, loved seascapes. More, it enriches the personality type. Some information will be checkable which is wonderful to be able to consolidate the information given. But good or bad information can be used to help research for evidence of this person.

How many times do we find ourselves thinking in a negative way, over-thinking, worrying that something bad will happen? We predict failures or disastrous situations before they even happen. This type of negativity will is powerful if left and can continue throughout and into the next lifetime, so with new information now, it would make sense to unravel those complexities of emotions and to deal with them.

Being a Victim

We have just touched lightly on how difficult patterns of behaviour can carry out through time but one scenario that emerges frequently is when someone has been a victim and understandably these memories can be particularly painful. These sessions may also take longer for the information to materialise and for the influx of images and patterns to start to make any sense. The theme of victimisation can result in fears of abandonment or of being misunderstood or blamed falsely, but whatever the cause this sense of sadness replays over and over.

It does take a certain bravery to be able to dig deep and to discover these terrible situations after all, the depth of emotion is still present and it can be difficult to find out that you have been a victim or, the perpetrator to any crime. And yet it is likely that there will be aspects of this in each and every one of us. It certainly takes maturity and bravery to be able to face up to difficult actions that may have been done in the past. The good news is that whatever the outcome of any of the sessions, it just takes an honest approach and an open mind to be able to understand that this information is given to help prevent these actions from happening again.

It is not about taking extreme action - going from victim to perpetrator, rather, it is about seeking out the true purpose in life, inviting in harmonious balance and living life to the full without negative extremes. The information becomes a tool for the individual to use as they need but whether they serve to analyse in-depth and then break free from negative patterns going forward is up to them, but a past life regression at the very least offers a great deal of comfort in that there is life after death.

It's always important to realise that each individual has the power to make positive and informed choices. No one has to play the victim or the perpetrator in life, with emotional intelligence comes awareness and the opportunity to break free from any negative energy patterns. Within each lifetime, there are multiple choices and of course, any decisions made will set new patterns – hopefully positive ones.

Actions that have been so significant in one lifetime can certainly be strong enough to impact future lifetimes and it is only by exposing the core of the problem that old patterns can be broken and new healthy patterns set.

Many people who have decided to seek out the truth of any potential past lives have discovered that there are a lot of unresolved issues lurking in their life. Instead of spending time dealing with problems as they have occurred these unresolved issues become dormant stagnating but eventually re-emerge bringing back destructive problems from time to time. Sometimes the smallest indicator of negativity can represent a traumatic experience in a former life.

Suicide

We all know that sometimes the path through life is far from easy and some people seem to suffer an extraordinary amount - family losses, grief or ill health and, it's hard for them to ope with the bombardment of difficulties that plague them. Sometimes, they take the only option they feel is open to them.

When people commit suicide, this does not stop them from continuing on their path of learning just because they have given up, there will still be things that they need learn. It may be that in subsequent lifetimes, this individual will still have to face unpleasant difficulties until those lessons have been learned. It's all about facing up to problems and learning to deal with them. So suicide does not break the contract of life and is not the easy way out after all.

Unfortunately, no-one is fully aware just what their true purpose in life is and so there is always the need to strive forward and to discover the full remit of that identity, why we are here and the ultimate purpose. By dipping into our past lives, it is possible to gain a better understanding of how those former lives panned out and this information can greatly increase the potential for success in this life and any lives going forward. Our purpose may be to overcome adversity, to strengthen will and to develop greater courage in life but one thing is certain, suicide does not stop the process, it merely resets the milestones.

In many ways, for all who believe in reincarnation, it can be a comfort to know that any family member or friend that has taken their lives will at least be reborn and get a chance to live their life out in full next time.

Chapter Eight

The Process

Every past life regression therapist has their individual way of commencing the session but the end goal will always remain the same. The goal is to relax the client and to start a journey of discovery opening up the potential for proof of past existences.

The process will vary largely due to the therapist intuitively assessing the client especially in the first session as those clients who are nervous may need to relax into a general hypnosis trance first and the regression session may be delayed somewhat. Complete trust can take time to build up and some client's may have turned to regression as more than a way of looking into the past, but as a way of talking through issues in the present – although these may be borne from a place of history.

The number of sessions booked will also vary depending on the ease of the regression session for example:

- Is the client open-minded with no preset perceptions of outcome?
- Is the client prepared to take time to seek out the truth about any former lives or has the session been booked out of curiosity?

Sometimes more than one session is required to drive to the root source of any issues or to reveal in-depth information about a former life, so time should always be allocated and it is up to he therapist to guide the client in this matter. If you consider that any behavioural patterns are likely to have developed over many years, it's understandable to consider that it may take some essions before the crux of any issue can be discovered and then brought to life.

Clients are encouraged to relax on a couch or in a chair, but the most important aspect initially is for them to feel comfortable and at peace. There is bound to be a little nervousness, this is understandable, but they are always encouraged to discuss their aims as to the session and to be open about any issues or concerns in their current life. This is not to help fuel a potential storyline but rather to help the therapist guide the client throughout and to be aware of any fears or triggers to look out for when the client is in trance state. This open communication also forges a stronger connection of trust between both. Rapport is extremely important within past life therapy regression, it cannot be hurried but the client must feel confident and comfortable throughout. Indeed they should be made aware that they are in charge the whole way through and although the therapist guides them through the process, supporting them, the clients may speed up the process or slow it down at any point.

It's also good to give the client a breakdown of what to expect before starting. The client needs to understand that the subconscious mind cannot analyse or form judgements of any former events, rather it is experienced as if happening in the present and if you consider that the memory, root behaviours and emotions come through the subconscious mind, it is easy to see that much can be revealed sometimes unexpectedly but certainly without analysis. The therapist has to get beyond the conscious mind and into the subconscious because the conscious mind can act as a barrier preventing progress. The therapist is non-judgemental and the client must be too.

Some clients may struggle to stay within the trance because their desire to analyse what they are seeing and feeling can pull them out of the trance. It is far better to let the memories and the images seen play out as if watching a film and then to participate in a discussion-both clients and therapist afterwards. The therapist really acts as a guide helping the clients into a more favoured route usually through asking non-leading questions.

The therapist will use a favoured exercise to help progress the session in the first instance. This usually enables their client to turn their attention inwards and to be able to enter the trance state. For most people, this is a pleasurable part of hypnosis. As the client slips into a deeper trance, they are advised that they can share vocally any images that they see, or, to feel free to summarise throughout. Many people find it a comfort that they will be able to speak out and, to be heard.

Most people will remain completely aware of all that is going on throughout the whole process but there are a small percentage of people who go so deeply within the trance that they can forget all that they have seen, so the therapist generally has to be aware of this and to set the intention for the session.

There are various techniques which the therapist can use to take someone back through time and this includes the use of symbolic images or simply through recalling memories, going all the way back through their present life, familiarising themselves with each of these stages before moving backwards.

It is important that the client does not force any images or for them to think too deeply about any memory, the whole idea is that the memories or images drift into an easy conscious state without being forced. Utilising the senses while experiencing a scene or memory can be a very powerful way of engaging with it even more, for example:

- How do you feel?
- Describe any scents in the air.
- Describe the colours around you.

This helps the memories to open up and for the client to feel a part of the scene sometimes vividly and at other times, the memory may only form partially giving a mere glimpse into the scene. Eventually, the client will find the whole process familiar and will be confident with recalling these memories and at witnessing the impressions as they occur as they are regressed back to birth and then beyond. This is then known as moving between lives.

This can be an odd feeling, but one which is totally peaceful. Some people feel as if they are floating among the stars and others see colours, some people feel as if they are receiving instructions about their next steps, but, it's important to note that there is no right or wrong way to be in this space between time.

The therapist then guides the client into the next stage of the regression via any one of a number of suggested routes:

- Through a door
- A pathway
- Crossing a bridge
- Through a tunnel
- Ascending or descending stairs

This entry into a former life is of course symbolic but it helps with the transition.

The next stage is an exciting one as the client embarks upon a journey of discovery to find out who they were in a previous existence; some people are greeted with vivid imagery the moment they step into their former life, while others have to wait for the memories or scenes to form. It is different for everyone.

It is important to note that people can also take on the form of a different gender in a former life so being a woman in this one does not mean that the gender would be the same throughout. The therapist may prompt for a description, perhaps of clothes worn which can afford many clues as to time and place and it also fine-tunes the client's ability to give as much detail as possible. They may request a description of the physique too.

Gradually through careful questions, it is possible to establish a partial view of the person they once were by associating where they live, the type of place and even food that is eaten. Some clients become so involved with their memories, they can happily narrate with very little need for prompting but otherwise, the therapist can continue to ask questions to help the client feel fully aware of all that is happening around them and to ensure as much information returns from the other life as possible.

As regression sessions continue, it's possible to visit various times that were instrumental in that life, sometimes these memories are obtained chronologically but they can be accessed in order of importance or through free will. Even those clients' who struggle with the regression process initially, can suddenly be involved within a deeply complicated story whereby, these key events can suddenly provide detailed insight into that lifetime.

People tend to fear death - in any lifetime but the therapist can skilfully manoeuvre the client around the circumstances in a way that is completely safe, taking the clients' as close as possible, (perhaps a few moments before) so they can embrace those last moments and relish the thoughts experienced. Although this may sound fearful, there is usually a great sense of peace experienced following this and a unique understanding gained of that lifetime.

An important part of the regression process is to review all the information experienced afterwards, clients are reminded that there is no judgement at all, so irrespective of the information that arises from the session, it can be discussed without prejudice. This aids trust but is a wonderful way of helping to build up a picture of the personality in that former life. It may become apparent that their soul had a distinct purpose during that lifetime which may or may not have been achieved.

Deeply intense and satisfying experiences may occur through emotionally charged sad or happy events, it's all part of the fabric surrounding the past life experience. Some people report having met former friends or family members at that time, but who are now familiar in the present life. While others discover that they are still carrying elements of that life.

By going into a past life regression with an open mind, there is the potential to discover so many new and surprising elements to the persona of today and the personas of those former existences, the potential is staggering.

Regression also forms an integral part of any healing process. Perhaps in a former life there were actions carried out that were seemingly unforgivable, but in this lifetime, it's possible to let go of guilt, remorse or regrets of the past. Equally, a client may have been emotionally or physically hurt by someone in their former life and the pain through being unresolved has continued into the present, the action of letting go can be intense, emotional but can spark off the deep healing that is required.

For anyone who carries unresolved issues, cleansing is important as certainly forgiveness opens up the doorway towards positive experiences going forward with an ease of releasing the past and to learn from the experience. Some people find the whole process so beneficial that they sign up for more sessions so that they can learn more about their previous lives. This gives them a greater option for research and to clarify some of the lessons and to develop in their present life.

It's also important to note that in between sessions, those who enjoy daydreaming or who practice meditation may find other memories surge up unbidden and these new memories can add to the correlation between the present-day issues and the past. This can also be discussed at the next session. By having the past life regression session recorded, it gives the perfect opportunity to review the recording and to provide the opportunity for expression thereafter.

Once the initial steps have been made into a past life, it is far easier to embark upon future sessions which may reveal drastically different values, emotions and experiences or to provide new messages for development based upon the previous life. It's a wonderful opportunity to be able to return to a past life with a view of learning more and to aiding the healing process in the present.

If you decide to have a past life regression, you may experience a floating sensation which is your soul leaving your physical body. This often occurs when you are in between lifetimes. The experience can be a little unsettling but know that the therapist is there to guide you. It's a type of sensation experienced when near death or when someone experiences astral projection.

It can take a few sessions before you feel fully confident and when in between lifetimes, you will be able to settle into the experience rather than to fight it. It does give you the opportunity to absorb information and to understand that you can enter the trance-like state easily and, can also return to conscious reality when desired. This helps you to feel more relaxed in this in-between state.

What is your soul's purpose?

Most people feel the need to understand what their purpose in life is. It's the age-old question of why am I here. We all feel that there has to be a reason for our existence, so by finding our true purpose in life or by understanding the reality of the present, it can give a profound sense of importance to the here and now.

If you have ever felt uncertain of your direction in life or felt trapped by low self-esteem or have felt unable to overcome limitations in life, then stepping back in time to discover the root cause of those issues or just to answer any questions you may have about your former life, it can help to redefine who you are now. Just remember that you are a product from your past. If you consider that reincarnation equate to our souls being reborn in new bodies and that we learn lessons as we progress, it makes sense that we still have an intrinsic link to the past, that it affects the present and the future too.

It's not about searching for perfection but rather, past life therapy can be all about discovering the real you, that unique individual who is swayed in the fluctuating uncertainty of time and can be overwhelmed and hampered by the obstacles in life. A lack of confidence, self doubts, obsessive behaviours, eating disorders, anger issues or anxiousness may all occur through aspects of a former life. A past life is not guilty of overshadowing your present remember that you are responsible for all that happens in life, but a journey back to the past can certainly answer a lot of questions.

We are everything that we strive to be, but the memories of the soul may stretch back many centuries. Sometimes we react instinctively or in accordance with a situation, at other times, our response can be shaped by circumstances unknown to us.

However you act in life now, it will be partly formed through experiences in this lifetime and certainly experiences gained in a former life. Every single experience brings knowledge but it can also create problems when we are unsure of how to respond. Some people are stuck in karmic patterns that they have not yet learned how to resolve, others are more than greatly influenced by past experiences but may not have realised it yet, and you may have discovered your connection to one former life and now may be on the journey to learn more.

Open your eyes and perspective and be ready to experience and embark upon this journey of discovery.

Knowledge gives you the opportunity to continue on the same route in life, but it also gives you the opportunity to avoid making mistakes, neatly side-stepping established patterns of behaviour. It's good to know that negative past life experiences can turn into positive experiences in the present, so even negativity can benefit at some point.

Many people are greatly drawn towards discovering past lives and it is a wonderful experience irrespective of what you learn. After the session, it's possible to make sense of everything learned. Seeing the bigger picture and identifying a sea of faces, impressions and indefinable images is never easy but the effort is worth it.

It may be that in a former life you failed to meet your true potential through your own inaction or as a result of someone else's actions against you. If you stepped back further in time, did the same happen then? This could be a cycle consistently repeated and so it's important to change this in the present. The route to your true purpose may be littered with obstacles but it may only take an adaptation of behavioural patterns right now to enable you to progress further along that route.

But past life regression is not all about negative elements from the past although even those bad elements can be put to good use in the present. By utilising hypnosis, you will be able to communicate with your unconscious mind through trance and you may be out to discover unique elements that can be updated and prepared for your present lifetime. The memories of your soul are available, you simply need to communicate with your unconscious mind and this is where past life regression therapy opens up the door to your past.

Whispers from the past

With the awareness of past life regression therapy, you may find more and more information surfaces, and you are more likely to take this information seriously than if you were not open-minded about reincarnation. Whether you believe fully that this information comes as a result of accessing your former life, you should still consider them. It's important to remember that you have the opportunity to discover the truth when you step back into a former life and the process of doing so is exciting and safe.

We cannot spend all our time in the past, we all have to make as much as possible of our present lives, but it does make sense to bring awareness of the past into this life, to strengthen it and to guide. But we cannot remain there; the journey is to strengthen the potential for the here and now and of course, to make the pathway to the future a smoother one. With this in mind, you will take a more grounded approach to this journey of discovery.

Chapter Nine

Questions

If you are still uncertain whether to seek out the services of a past life therapist, take time to read the following questions and answers as these should quell any doubts holding you back. The following are general questions asked before a past life regression session begins:

Is it possible to become stuck in a past life?

The good news is that it is not possible to become stuck in a past life however; it is true to say that the experience of coming close to death in the session may seem so strong that it takes just a few moments to adjust to being back in your conscious reality afterwards. But if you think about it, this is little different than when being totally absorbed in a favourite book or film. It may be a slightly disconcerting sensation of being jerked back into reality while the remnants of the feelings of the former life stay with you, but these moments are fleeting.

The therapist will help you to ease back into your conscious mind slowly and this will help you to adjust far more readily to your true reality. Although you will not become stuck in a past life, you may find that the intensity of the experience remains with you for some time afterwards. This is not a bad thing, because you are opening the doorway to former lives during the regression and when you become confident and relaxed within the sessions, you will know that it is easy to slip back into your conscious state. You are in control after all.

Did I just imagine the whole thing?

It's understandable for anyone visiting a past life regression therapist for the very first time to consider if the whole thing really happened or whether the information came from their imagination. It's important to consider what is the source of your imagination in which case? So any images that you experienced - were they from a film that you have seen or a book that you have read?

It can be difficult to answer these questions because you are not trying to cheat in the session you want the truth and your unconscious mind will have a link to the stimulus from this life. It certainly can help to have more than one past life regression session, simply because it may not give enough information initially or, if the information was largely muddled or intense. It is highly unlikely that your imagination would play a role in this.

What if I can't be hypnotised?

Many people would like to be hypnotised and to undergo a past life regression session but there is often a feeling of anxiousness as to whether they can even be hypnotised. The good news is that it is a natural state and one that most people can achieve. The therapist is a guide who can help you ease into the state easily. There is however a small percentage of people who will not be hypnotised and these include:

- Those people who are on prescribed medication or drugs that serve to alter the function of the brain
- Young children and babies
- Those under the influence of alcohol or drugs
- Those who are determined to resist the hypnosis process.

There is some indication to say that those who have a good imagination or who are willing to cooperate and follow the instructions are easier to hypnotise than others.

Will I lose control of my mind?

It may seem daunting to be in a trance but the good news is that the therapist does not take control of your mind. You will always have complete control and cannot be made to do anything that you do not want to.

What if I want to come out of hypnosis?

It doesn't matter how deeply hypnotised you are, if there is an emergency or you feel the need to come back to your conscious reality, you can do so at any time.

Will I forget everything that occurs within the session?

Some people are concerned that they will forget everything that was said or seen within the sessions and although it can happen, it's good to know that this is only likely to happen to a very small percentage of those who seek out a past life therapy regression. As sessions can be recorded, there is little need for concern.

Will I remember death?

We are potentially all a little squeamish at the prospect of our own death. After all, there's no pleasant way to know that the end is coming, but for those who believe in past life regression, it offers a great deal of comfort in that death is not the end. This gives the opportunity to be able to view any death relating to a former life objectively, so instead of it being horrific as one might expect, it actually becomes a relief.

The therapist will guide the client as close as possible to be able to gain all the impressions of that time as these are facts which are checkable. In this stage of the regression, people have reported hovering above their bodies and looking down at themselves in the same way that people in the present life describe a near death moment. But the therapist can move them to the point where instead of feeling fear, there is a sense of peace and understanding.

Can Past Lives explain contradictions in our heart and minds? E.g. have a natural passion/ interest in something that contradicts with my conscious mind/ beliefs, which results in feeling confused/ hypocritical?

Yes it could be connected to a Past Life. So, it may be that you have a passion in something like horses and want to make a living from that, but you feel confused because your belief system tells you that you should not do that, you should go and get a regular job that pays a regular income – i.e. office job for example. You may have had a number of lives in the past where you have had a special connection with horses and that passion is with you, but so is the contradiction. However, the belief system may well be from this lifetime but perhaps one of your karmic lessons in this lifetime is to break free from expectations of you, so therefore the passion for the horses is stronger than ever.

Can we be in more than one life at the same time?

Yes it is possible! There are theories and clients have reported living parallel lives at the same time in different locations - and then of course the quantum physics - are all lives being played out together - past, present, future?! It's a mind blowing subject!

Why do some people have so many drawbacks in life whilst others seem to just sail through?

It can seem challenging when you see that. In our Between Lives, we make choices about our upcoming life, so it may be that we chose a hard life to overcome some karma from the past. It is likely that we will have had easy lives previously too. It is all our own choice.

Have I had Past Lives with my family before – my son & husband?

It's quite possible that yes you have had past lives with close family members before. We sometimes reincarnate as different roles in each other's lives – so your son could have previously been your father, your husband could have been your daughter....very often they are different roles but we will share the life with them.

Chapter Ten

Case Studies

In this section, I've included real life case studies to give you a greater insight into past life regression. Each story is unique and very real and I am grateful to these clients for allowing me to share their stories with you.

A Story of the Titanic

As it has been a significant anniversary in the last few years of the sinking of the Titanic, this reminded me of a clients experience when she was regressed during a Past Life Regression group workshop. Not very often does a client come in and have a story that is linked to someone or something famous but that happened to have been the case here.

Here is what she had to say about what she discovered.

"During my course with yourself as you know I saw me as a little girl, maybe 5 or 6. I was playing on a hill by some water. It was very green. I remember my father calling me and swinging me up into his arms and myself giggling. He called me Lizzy but no one else did, not even my mum. I am not sure why I remembered that detail. I then saw myself on a ship – a large ship. I was in my early 20's. I spent most of the time in my room, a room where I spent a lot of time alone and crying.

I don't know why I was crying but I feel I was running from something. I was on my own and I didn't know anyone. The next thing I knew I was in water, cold water. It was so cold that even when I came back from the experience I was cold. I had goose bumps on my arm from being cold. While I was in the water I knew I was going to die. Everyone around me was screaming and throwing their arms and legs around. Mothers, children, there were people everywhere. I just closed my eyes and that's all I saw.

After I knew it was the Titanic. I didn't at first say it was. I just told them about the water as I was concerned I that I imagined the image in my head. I told of the hills and the cold water, and my sadness on the boat. After everyone had gone through theirs, I still had the shivers from being cold and I knew what I saw was truly my previous life. I came home quite excited about the past life as it explained a few things.

When I watched the movie Titanic before I went to Karen's course, I had always had odd reactions. I always got very angry and cried during the parts where the third class passengers were locked. I very rarely watched the whole movie.

A few months went by and as life takes over things the past life experience was filed into the back of my head. One day, many months down the road, my husband and I were talking about if we could afford for me to go back to the course when Karen was coming back to Manchester. This got my daughter thinking and she asked me some questions about my past life that I remembered. I told her the details I did know :like my name was Elizabeth, I was Irish, I was in my early to mid 20's I was in 3rd class and was running away from something bad.

She went onto a website (I don't know why I never thought to do this) and after an hour or so said 'Mum do you think you might have been 24?' I just told her yes without even thinking about it. She then told me there was an Elizabeth Doyle who was 24 and from Ireland. As soon as she said that name, I got chills and started crying. I knew at that moment that was my past life name.

This is the most amazing experience and it helped me I think to let go some of that tragedy and I believe still that my aura is a bit better to unload some of those past demons.

I look forward to learning about some more of my previous lives………."

Anne's Story

Anne contacted me after the loss of her husband, still in the grieving process. After much discussion and when the time was right, we met and began the first of a series of Regressions which explored Past Lives, Life Between Lives & Future Lives for Anne.

A beautiful caring soul who at a time of great sadness began her inner journey and that journey still continues today. You will read from Anne's own words how many of her past lives have ended and it could be that this could have happened again, but the loss of her husband sent Anne's life in a completely different direction.

Now in her early 70's, Anne counsels other people, is a qualified Hypnotherapist and Regression therapist and uses her own experiences to help people of all different ages deal with life's events.
All those years ago from the very first email that I received, I had no idea the learning I would receive from Anne.

Her own personal journey and soul has been shared with me on numerous occasions and she now wonderfully volunteers to come along to my Regression trainings so my students can understand, learn and hear of Anne's story through time. I have been very blessed to have her as a client and am in awe of someone who has broken the cycle of ending their lives and is now helping so many others. Thank you Anne.

Here is Anne's story in her own words:

After the loss of my beloved husband and soul mate, I was in a place of complete and utter despair and hopelessness. All I wanted was to be with him wherever he was. I could not see a life beyond the pain and blackness that engulfed me.

I felt I had a heart full of love to give and no one to share it with. It was at this point that I believe I was guided to the books of Michael Newton and from there to a remarkable hypnotherapist, Karen who I have been privileged to work with on a number of occasions.

In many of the past lives I visited, I suffered the same despair, loneliness and longing which eventually led me to being responsible for the ending of my own life. In isolating myself in grief and sadness, I had wasted my life and turned away from my soul's need to love and be loved.

It was a life changing realisation. At the age of 65, I went back to college and qualified as a counsellor and hypnotherapist. In my work as a humanistic counsellor, I support and counsel many individuals and groups who are grieving or who have suffered bereavement through suicide and individuals who are themselves suicidal. I know this is where I am meant to be. This is where I am most fulfilled. Maybe I got it right this time…..

Relationship Issues

Hazel is a journalist who at the time was going to have a Past Life Regression session with me over Skype to promote my sessions and workshops in Dublin, Ireland. Because she had agreed to write an article on me, I hoped the session went well and as you will read, it did!

Here is the article that Hazel wrote:

For years, I have been very interested in past life regression (PLR). I have never doubted that all of us have been here on earth before and that our souls are learning lessons in every life time. One lifetime alone could not teach us all we need to know!

I had my first experience of PLR in Singapore in the early 1990s. I found it very empowering and very interesting – especially when I was able to verify, through contact with a Welsh university – that the person I had remembered being had actually existed!

Over the years since then, I have had a few formal regression sessions as well as a number of spontaneous rememberings. Initially, I used to wonder how to tell the difference between an 'imagining' and a real past life memory. Thankfully, I have discovered that differentiating between the two is not at all difficult. Imagination takes 'effort', while the memories of a previous life arise spontaneously. Also, they are often the kinds of things my imagination could never invent! Critically, though, my body experiences past life memories and the workings of my imagination differently.

'   How people experience memories from past lives varies. Often, I find that the experience depends on how they think,' Karen E Wells, a Past Life Regression therapist, explains. 'If a person is very visual, they will see everything. Other people might have a hazy picture and have a sense of feeling the experience.'

'What makes it real is the feelings and the emotions and sometimes it can be a very intense experience. That's what lets you know that it's real,' Karen further explains. 'The conscious mind is so powerful that it will often come in and say "you're making that up". Forget what you think you think and go on what you feel.'

While I first investigated PLR as a matter of curiosity, I am now more likely to seek PLR in order to obtain clarification of a current circumstance, or a deeper explanation of a current relationship. Having experienced PLR therapists from various parts of the globe – as well as *in* various parts of the globe – I consider myself pretty hard to impress.

Last week, however, I was amazed by a session I had with Karen, who is based in the UK – but in Dublin at the end of November. When she's here, she will run a past life workshop, as well as to conduct consultations with individuals.

The difference between Karen's approach and the approach of the eight or nine other PLR therapists I have encountered is that Karen is clear about her use of PLR to heal. Karen herself says 'Past Life Regression can be a really amazing healing opportunity. Sometimes, when something is going on in someone's current life, the roots are in a past life. It is necessary to go o the time in the past life when the difficulty first arose and heal it there. Once there is clarity around the issue in that life, it will often heal in this current life. The issue can be physical, emotional or both.'

Much to my surprise, I encountered just such a healing when I had my own session with Karen. When regressed, I visited myself in another life – Egypt during the Ottoman times. In that lifetime, I was married – against my will – to a man I wanted nothing to do with. To cut a long story short, he was very cruel and I decided he had to die. With the help of an apothecary, I slowly poisoned my husband and he died. I became aware of who that person has reincarnated as in this life – and he has made a lot of trouble for me, to the extent that I am currently locked in a legal battle with him.

Coming towards the end of that session, Karen asked me if there was anything that was said in that lifetime – any promise or feeling – that had carried on into this lifetime.

'Yes,' I told her. 'He said, "I'll get you for this" just before he died.'

Suddenly, I had clarity around the issue in my current life. I realised that I had been feeling guilty and carrying that guilt with me for centuries. That guilt was part of the reason that had allowed this man to treat me so badly in this lifetime – on some level I felt that I deserved . At the same time, though, I was able to see that the karmic debt had been repaid in that lifetime itself; he had behaved terribly and had paid the price – I had killed him.

It was over and done with and I had no reason to feel guilty about pursuing satisfaction through legal channels for the harm he has done me in this lifetime. To put it simply, we were quits at the end of that life in Egypt and the slate was wiped clean. What happened in this lifetime needs to be dealt with here and now.

The session with Karen, however, helped me to realise – on a very conscious level – that don't deserve what was done to me in this life by the person in question, that I have every right to pursue things through legal channels, and that I am entitled to satisfaction for what happened.

The relief I felt at the end of the session was huge. I felt as though I could relax about the issue for the first time ever. I also believed with every part of my being that I deserve to have the legal resolution I am seeking to the issue.

Interestingly, the Universe seems to have realised that I have made that change – as things have sped up considerably in the legal arena of the issue. It now appears as though I will have a satisfactory outcome within the next few weeks. Which, when you consider that I was originally told it could take up to three years, is not bad going?

Follow-Up to Hazel's Story

When I consulted Karen, I was having mixed feelings about a situation with my brother and how it was developing. The information I gleaned from my consultation with Karen showed me that the approach I was taking was the right one – not just for me, but for my brother as well. He made an appearance in the past life that confirmed for me that, karmically, we still had a power tussle to sort out and by standing up to him; I was honouring myself in this life and also finishing a karmic agreement that had been playing out for centuries. I was also delighted to see my eldest daughter pop up in that life and I was amused to see where the seeds of certain elements of our current relationship were planted: The sense of familiarity and continuity was comforting (even though our relationship was a very different one in that life).

Firmly believing that while past lives are interesting, the only life that truly *matters* is the one you're living right now. Therefore, when Karen instructed my hypnotised self to bring a message/clarity from that life to this, it struck me as a very sensible thing to do.

The regression that I had with Karen left me feeling empowered and energised; more than merely being a bit of fun, this session was useful and informative. The issue with my brother resolved recently and I was very much at peace with both the resolution and the way it was achieved.

Letting Go To Move Forward….A Story of Successful Conception!

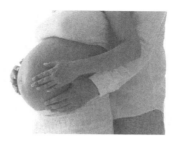

Regression can be so powerful in many ways. The greatest challenge to the hypnotherapist is the presenting issue that the client has – how do we solve it? How can my skills enable this client to move forward & achieve want she wants to achieve…? Here we see exactly how when regressing a client back to the origin of her issue, amazing things can appen……

A few years ago, a wonderful lady came to me with a fertility Issue. She had tried and tried for years to get pregnant and just hadn't been able to. The Doctor's had done all kinds of tests on her and her husband and medically she was told there was no reason she shouldn't be able to conceive…..

At the point the client came to see me, she had undergone 2 unsuccessful IVF treatments. She desperately wanted to have a child but was at her wits end.

After talking extensively to her, I decided to regress the client to the root cause of her infertility.

She went to a past life of hers and the memory that came was when her mother in that life had died. She felt that she had closed herself down emotionally at that point as she had to look after her youngest sister and deal with all the formalities of arranging the funeral. A lot of emotion was released at that time as she realised that she had never grieved for her mother and in seeing that memory she also realised that she was holding on to the thought that she couldn't bear to lose anyone close to her again.

She had therefore lived the rest of that life in isolation without marrying or getting close to anyone again.

After doing some healing work with the client around the memory and enabling her to release that emotion, we spoke afterwards and it became clear how she had held onto those feelings of not wanting to lose anyone she was close to. It finally dawned on her: Those feelings that emotion – everything from that point she felt had been stopping her from conceiving a child in this life.

It was a huge relief for my client to see that and to feel it. Could it really be that the reason she hadn't conceived was because she was scared of losing someone close to her again even though in this life she had married but had not been able to conceive?

She went away, knowing that in another 2 weeks she was to have her 3rd IVF treatment. asked her to keep in touch and let me know how it went…..a few weeks later I received a telephone call from my now very excited client, telling me she was pregnant at last and she really felt that the regression had helped her to release what she had held onto all that time and move on. 9 Months later a beautiful baby girl was born……..

Experiencing The Past In The Present Moment…..

Experiencing The Past In The Present Moment. How can something from a Past Life affect us in that way?

To understand this, we have to understand that we are more than just our physical bodies Physically & energetically, our cells, organs & energy bodies are full of every thought, feeling and experience that we have gone through in this lifetime and our past lives. We carry energy from our past lives with us so that we can clear these karmic lessons and patterns in this lifetime.

Here's an amazing account of one of the most powerful Past Life Sessions I have facilitated......

A Gentleman came to see me for a Past Life Regression in the hope he could find some answers to his Chronic Back Pain issue that he had been experiencing for years. He had been to see his doctor, a chiropractor, an osteopath, an acupuncturist and every alternative therapist he could think of. Nothing could help to relieve the pain he felt. He had done the rounds medically and as a Past Life Therapist I was his last hope!

When he came to see me, he was in so much pain that he could not sit in my therapy chair; he couldn't lie on my therapy couch, so the session took place with my client lying on the floor. We began the session and I regressed him back to the source of the pain – the root of where the pain originated from – and he found himself in a Past Life of his – in a battle field in the 16th century in England.

His pain seemed to then become more intense as he described being on the losing side in the battle and founding himself being held down by five men, one of which then placed a long sword in his back – in the exact area of where his current chronic back pain resided.

Guiding him gently through the experience whilst enabling him to have the expression that he was never able to experience in that Past Life, minutes later the back pain just disappeared!

When my client first walked into my office, his back pain was so bad he was unable to sit in a chair or lie on a therapy bed – he could only just manage to lie on the floor. At the end of the session, 95% of the pain had disappeared and after following up with him a few months later, all pain had gone and never returned!

It just goes to show how powerful Past Life Regression can be! Sometimes simply going back to the source of the issue, followed by healing techniques can shift the energy causing pain from hundreds of years ago!

The client knew exactly why this pain was being carried from the events he experienced in his Past Life...and simply letting that go and allowing expression now enabled a deep part of him to be healed. Incredible!

Back To Mayan Times – A Story Of Continuing Karma

2012 was such a significant year in many ways, particularly with the prophecies of the Mayan culture. I recently regressed a client back to one of their past lives and what came up was a life from the Mayan times....

The Mayan's existed approx 1800 years BC to 250 AD, so to see some issues still affecting my client today was quite an insight for them. Not wanting to look at any particular issue, I regressed my client back to a Past Life of theirs that was significant to their current life today.

The scene that presented itself was of a strong man who had quite a significance in his tribe (my client is female in this life) He was leaving his tribe after a disagreement, he felt like he had had enough and wanted to go off on his own.

His stubbornness really came through in that life and a feeling of wanting to be away from everyone and just live by himself. He was leaving behind a wife and his whole spiritual family. His only companion was a large cat – like a tiger or jaguar that had been constantly by his side his whole life. He felt that he valued this companion more than this wife, more than his tribe, more than anything.

The other members of the tribe looked on, knowingly that this stubbornness would lead to his downfall. The next scene showed exactly that. A short while after leaving the tribe, his companion – this large cat, turned on him and killed him. The feelings of being crushed in the back were really being felt physically at this point.

Using healing techniques, the pain went but the knowledge of the stubbornness, the feeling of just wanting to go off remained with the client. It resonated with how she could be in her current lifetime as well as shedding light on certain characteristics in her current personal relationships too; having recognised the wife in the Mayan life as someone significant in her current life today.

What we can take from this Past Life Regression session is a sense of recognition of Karma, of characteristics being played out thousands of years later. To see that and to heal the energy from that time that still remains with us is powerful stuff!

The War Within.......

A client came to see me with a feeling of a deep connection to the World War 2 and to Russia. He found himself fascinated by both of these things and would watch as many TV programs as he could to further his interest. He came for a Past Life session to see if he had experienced a Past Life during one of those times.

When I regressed him back into a past life with this connection, he went to a scene in 1941 when he was in Russia as an Austrian soldier. He was a young lad about the age of 18, and the area was full of peasants and German trucks.

He had a sense that the soldiers had the right to take what they wanted, but deep down, deep within he knew it was wrong what was happening and didn't want to hurt anybody. We moved to the next scene and he was feeling very cold, with frostbite and hadn't been warm for weeks. The area he was in had been bombed; those soldiers that were left were now sleeping and eating in the rubble.

Some soldiers had even killed themselves.

Within 18 months, the Russians were fighting freely with even young children as young as 9 or 10 years old that had hate in their eyes. He said he felt that Hitler had bought death to the world and he knew this war could not be won by them.

Moving on, shortly after he had been killed, his last thoughts and feelings were that he felt so responsible for what he had done and what others had done but he did his duty. After some healing, he was able to see how in this current lifetime he was here to help people, no matter what their differences were and for the last few years things have awakened inside him to do just that.

It begs the questions: Have we all had past lives where we have done something we may have regretted? Are soldiers the result of their conditioning, the ego, the following of what they should do? Was the same happening in the young Russian children? What would happen if they really listened within....?

Are things any different then to how they are now in the wars in the world? Perhaps this Past Life had created a War Within for my client......

Chapter Eleven

Why You May Wish to Train in Past Life Regression

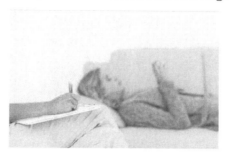

Having reached this stage of the book, you may be wondering whether there is the potential or a career in past life therapy regression and the good news is, that there is. Here are 10 reasons ɔ do Past Life Regression training:

1) To Expand Your Own Experience as A Therapist

Training in Past Life Regression offers many new skills for you and your clients to explore deep ssues that have been carried forward from their past lives into this lifetime.

2) Past Life Regression is a highly specialised field of Hypnotherapy.

More & More clients are turning within to explore themselves and you could be at the forefront f this amazing spiritual revolution!

3) Learn new specialised Skills – Regression Therapy is a Journey Back in Time.

ather than using suggestive therapy which has limited use & benefit, get to the deep rooted sues for your clients. Regression skills are needed to take them back to certain points & times rithin this and past lives. You can do this with Past Life Regression Training.

4) Resolve Your Clients Issues Effectively & Quickly.

There are amazing tools that are shared in the training, which allow you to very quickly and very effectively help resolve your client's issues and let them move forward in life.

5) **Gain Confidence & Expertise With The Amazing Tools That Past Life Regression Offers Your Clients**

There is no other therapy that takes your clients back to their past lives and lets them heal physical & emotional issues from so long ago. The tools in the training give you the confidence and the ability to do this for others.

6) **Open Yourself & Your Clients Up To Infinite Possibilities Of Space & Time**

Past Life Regression gives you and your clients the validation that this lifetime isn't "just it" Your clients may have had hundreds or thousands of lives, all this can be revealed to them and more when they undertake a Past Life Regression with you.

7) **Enable Your Clients To See & Know Who They Where In Previous Lives**

You will be easily taking your clients back to many past lives so they can see exactly who they were and what they were doing in their past lives. Each story is fascinating and you will be in the driver's seat taking them there!

8) **Explore The Healing Opportunities That Have Been Carried Over For Hundreds & Thousands Of Years**

Physical & Emotional issues are often found with their roots in past lives, meaning that for hundreds or thousands of years, your clients have been carrying these issues with them and you can now help them to heal and resolve them!

9) **Run Powerful One To One Sessions Or Group Workshops To Touch The Lives Of Those Coming Forward To Explore Their Own Immortality**

Your sessions with your clients can be run as a personal 1-2-1 with them or you will learn the skills of how to take groups into a regression, giving you the chance to touch more lives of those that want to explore this inner side.

10) Follow Your Life Purpose By Healing Others & Their Pasts

If you have a passion for past lives, it could be that its part of what you're here to do, helping others heal from their Past....

Summary

Hopefully now that you have finished this book, you will have retained and increased your interest in past life regression therapy, it's a fascinating subject and one that has such potential in terms of helping others and provides a satisfying career for therapists the world over. Perhaps you will decide to take your own journey into the past to discover who you were in a previous life, or, perhaps you will decide to help others by studying for a professional qualification that gives so much joy for all those who take the step from the present into the past.

At the very least, you will understand why so many people do seek out the services of a professional therapist in the aim of understanding themselves, all of their foibles or by discovering any unresolved issues that may taint the present time.

This is a therapy that continues to give. Long after the therapy sessions have concluded the memories and the deep connection to the past continues to come forth and it can provide a sense of peace in this life. It also offers those struggling to overcome issues to make informed choices, removing age-old obstacles and unlocking the secrets to their true potential. After all, by understanding just how you fared in your former lives, you can find reassurance in this one.

We all have the power to take the lessons earned and with wisdom, strive to make the present day as good as it can possibly be. With a clearer perspective and clarity, it opens up the potential to change and to encourage our own personal growth.

A past life regression can lift the veil on emotional or psychological disorders and to gain greater insight into any physical pain, any phobias or syndromes experienced. There is less guess-work in life, less disharmony or discord, in fact, there's greater peace of mind and confidence.

Past Life Regression enables you to explore former skills and to bring those rich element into the everyday – whether it is musical skills, creative, healing or sports prowess. Whatever th skill, it can be rediscovered and utilised to further the quest for development. In a spiritual sense egression can affect how you view the universe thereafter, because you gain a far greater understanding of the meaning of life and your place in it. There is a sense of peace that life after death exists and that we are all connected and intertwined and that those who we care about deeply now, that their souls will be reborn in a future life. It's only through exploration of the past can the present and future be enriched.

Whatever benefits you have gained through reading this book or through your future research, may the journey be kind.

Karen E. Wells

Karen's passion and interest has always been in past lives, exploring her own and wanting to help others do the same. Her journey into practical therapies started over 14 years ago and she trained in Hypnotherapy, Past Life Regression and Life Between Lives Regression. Seeing the huge gap needed in these therapies of healing, Karen continued her journey on numerous self development and healing courses with spiritual teachers Mike Robinson & Jo Le-Rose (www.mikerobinson.eu.com) (www.jolerose.solutions)

Karen's own inner journey enabled her to understand the human suffering within herself and others. Her unique experience and skills of the combination of Regression and Healing mean that each person that comes for a session begins and continues their own inner journey. She shows each individual the key to letting go of old patterns that have been set up through conditioning. A way to find inner freedom.

This is for those who are prepared to take the steps of finding the freedom for themselves.

After establishing a busy worldwide practice, Karen set up her own training academy - The KEW Training Academy to fill a gap in the market to teach other therapists the skills of regression and healing. This expanded into a full range of classroom & online courses in different subjects that make learning fun, educational and easy.

The KEW Training Academy offers easy and effective solutions that work for you either personally or professionally.

If you wish to explore your own past lives you can take advantage of a FREE Past Life Regression MP3 included with this book by clicking here: http://www.karenewells.co.uk/mp3s/ just enter code PLRBOOK to receive your free MP3.

For details of all of Karen's courses – click on the link; www.kewtrainingacademy.com

Image Credits

Past Life Regression

Exploring The Past to Heal The Present

Karen E Wells

Printed in Great Britain
by Amazon